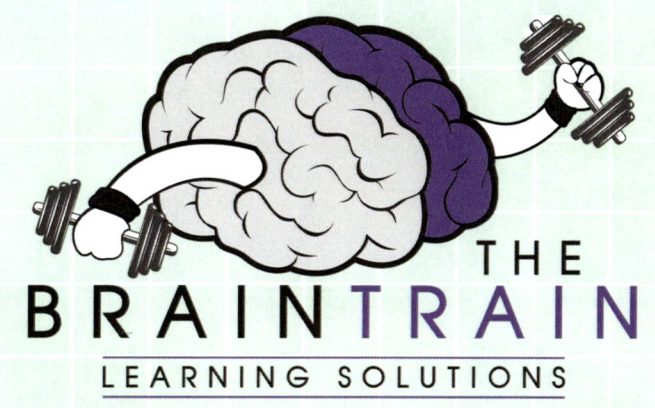

MY FREAKIN' AMAZING BRAIN!

The Brain Train Learning Solutions
My Freaking Amazing Brain!
copyright © 2023

All rights reserved. No part of this book may be reproduced or utilized in any form or by any means, electronic or mechanical, including photocopying, recording, or by any information storage and retrieval system, without written permission from the publisher.

LearningRx brain training has made a huge impact in hundreds of thousands of lives. Through this training program and methodology, many lives are changed. To learn more about brain training, visit **www.learningrx.com**

WHAT DOES YOUR BRAIN DO?

Your brain is an amazing organ that controls everything you think, all the ways you move, everything you see, hear, smell, and feel and it helps you remember to do all the things that you should and some things you don't want to remember.

WHAT IS YOUR BRAIN?

Your brain is an organ that functions like a muscle which needs exercise to get strong and to stay strong.

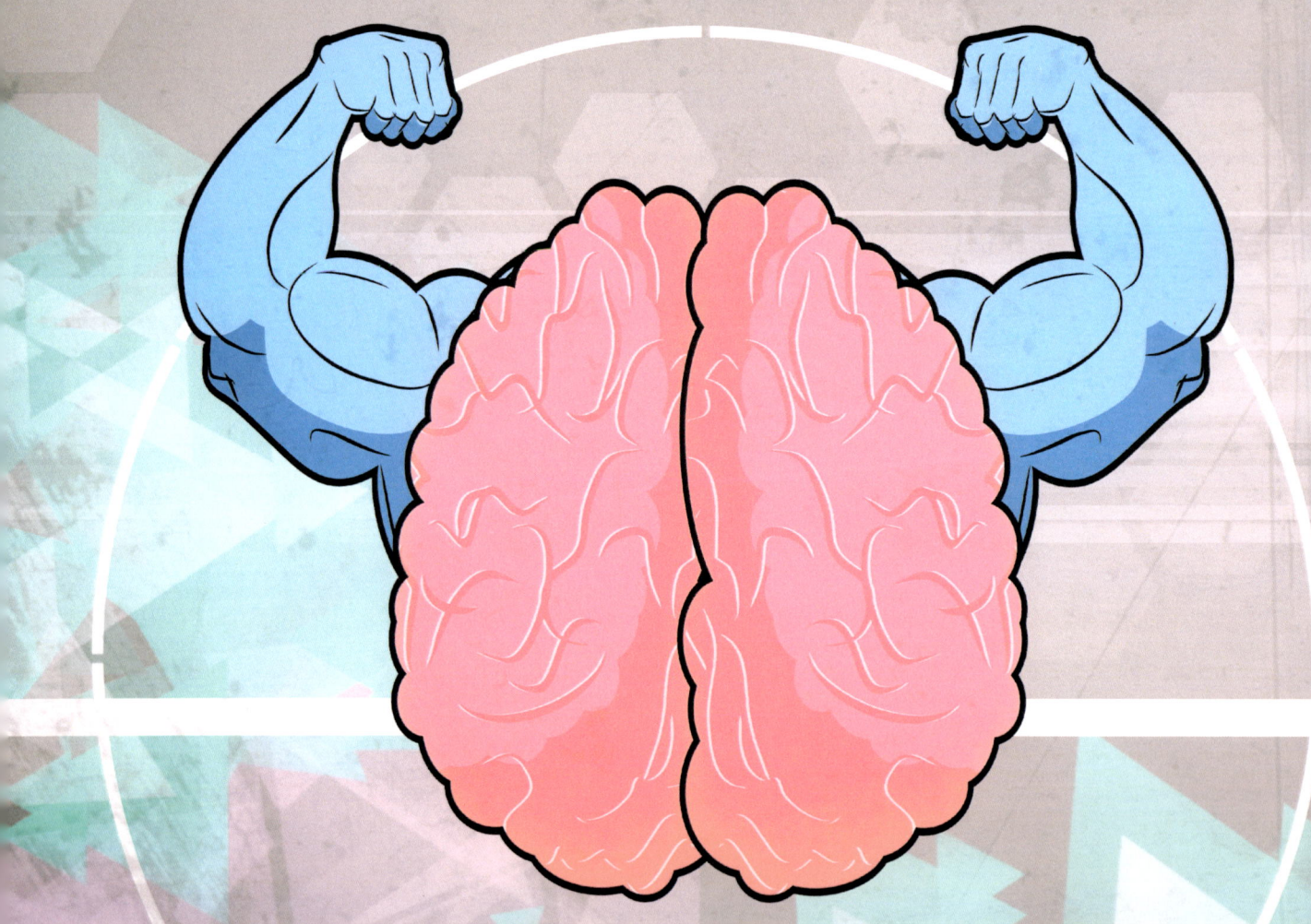

Like a runner trying to make their legs stronger by practicing, the more you use a certain skill, the better you become at that skill. If something is hard for you, it gets easier the more that you practice it.

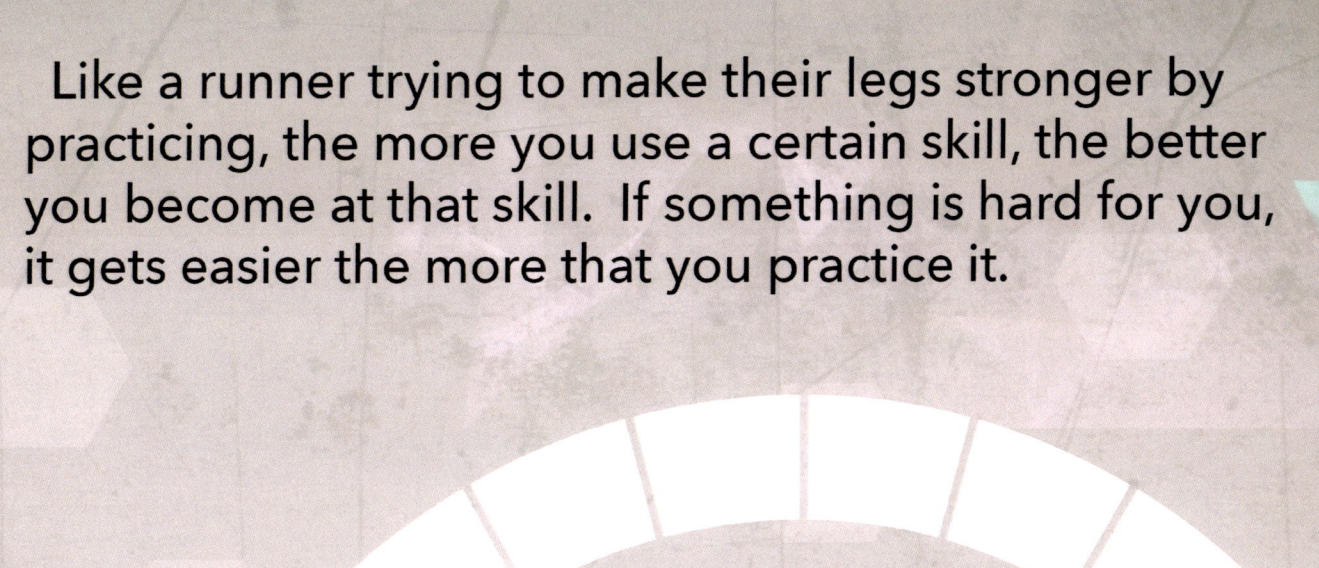

Some parts of your brain like the Cerebrum help you think or speak and other parts like your cerebellum help you move your body.

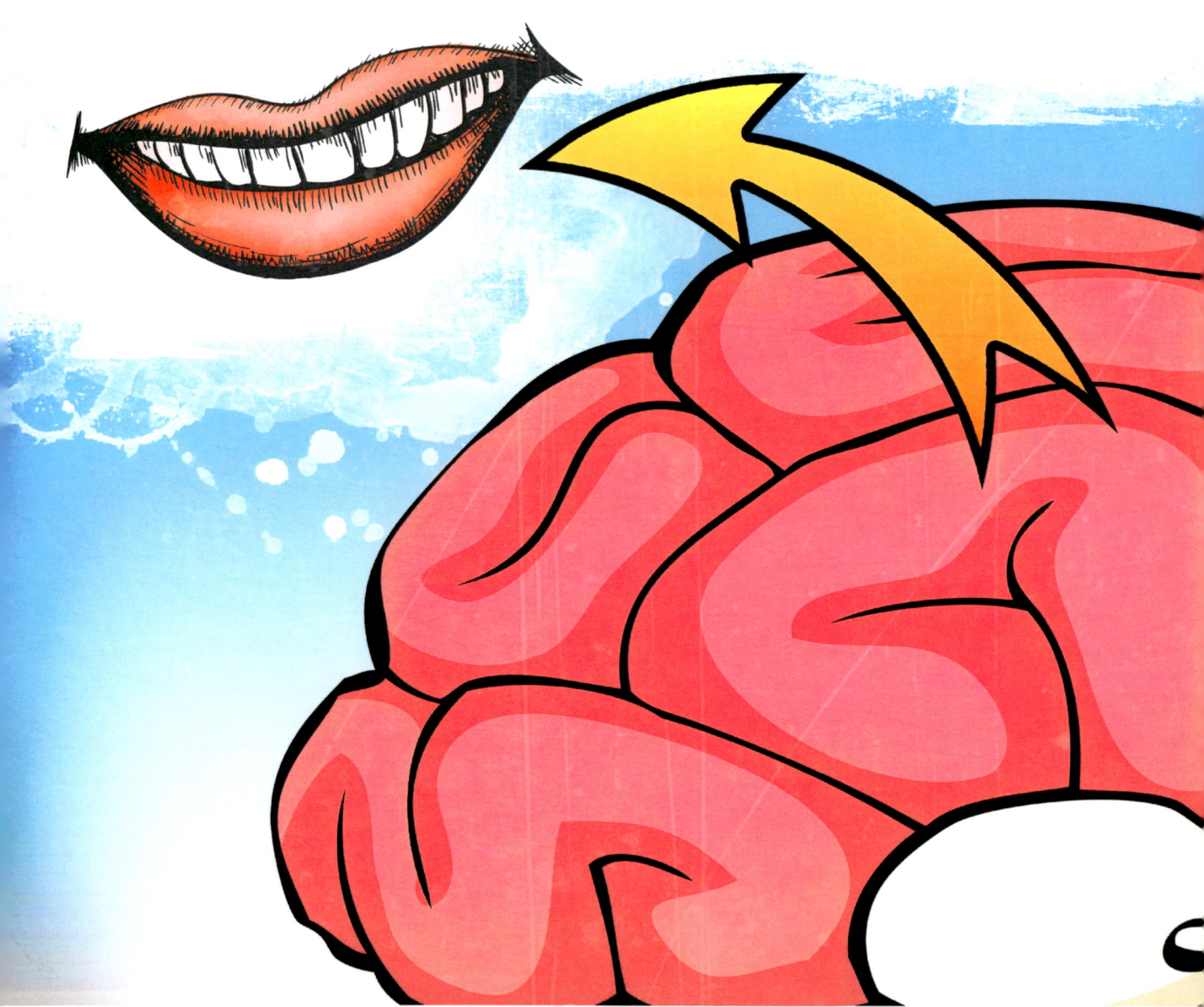

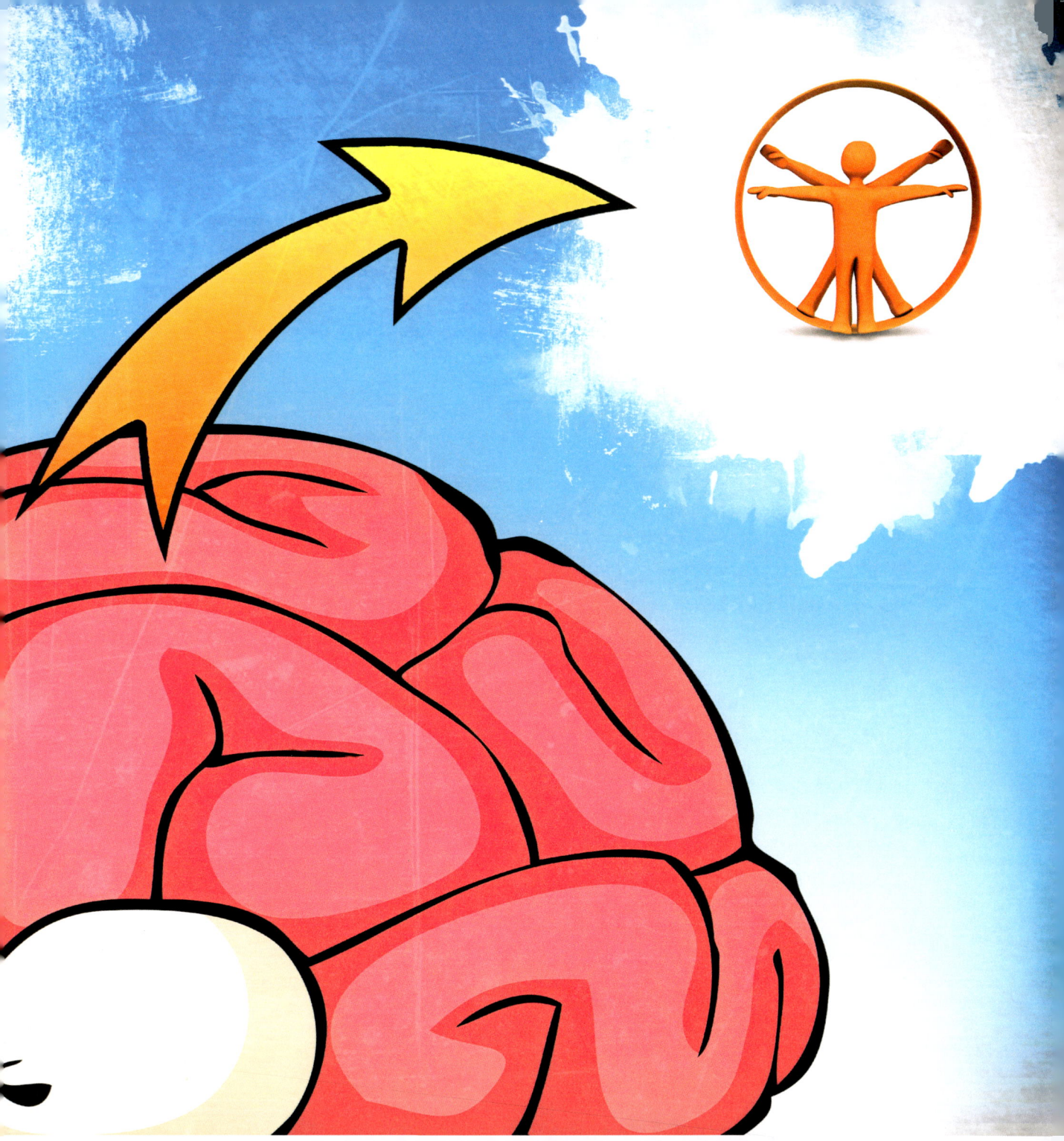

The front part of your brain that helps you plan and make decisions is called the prefrontal cortex while the part that controls your emotions is called the Amygdala.

The Hippocampus is the part of the brain that keeps up with all of your learned skills like a big memory bank of a giant computer. That is because all of the tiny brain cells called neurons are all around your brain and send electrical impulses like lightning bolts full of information all over the brain.

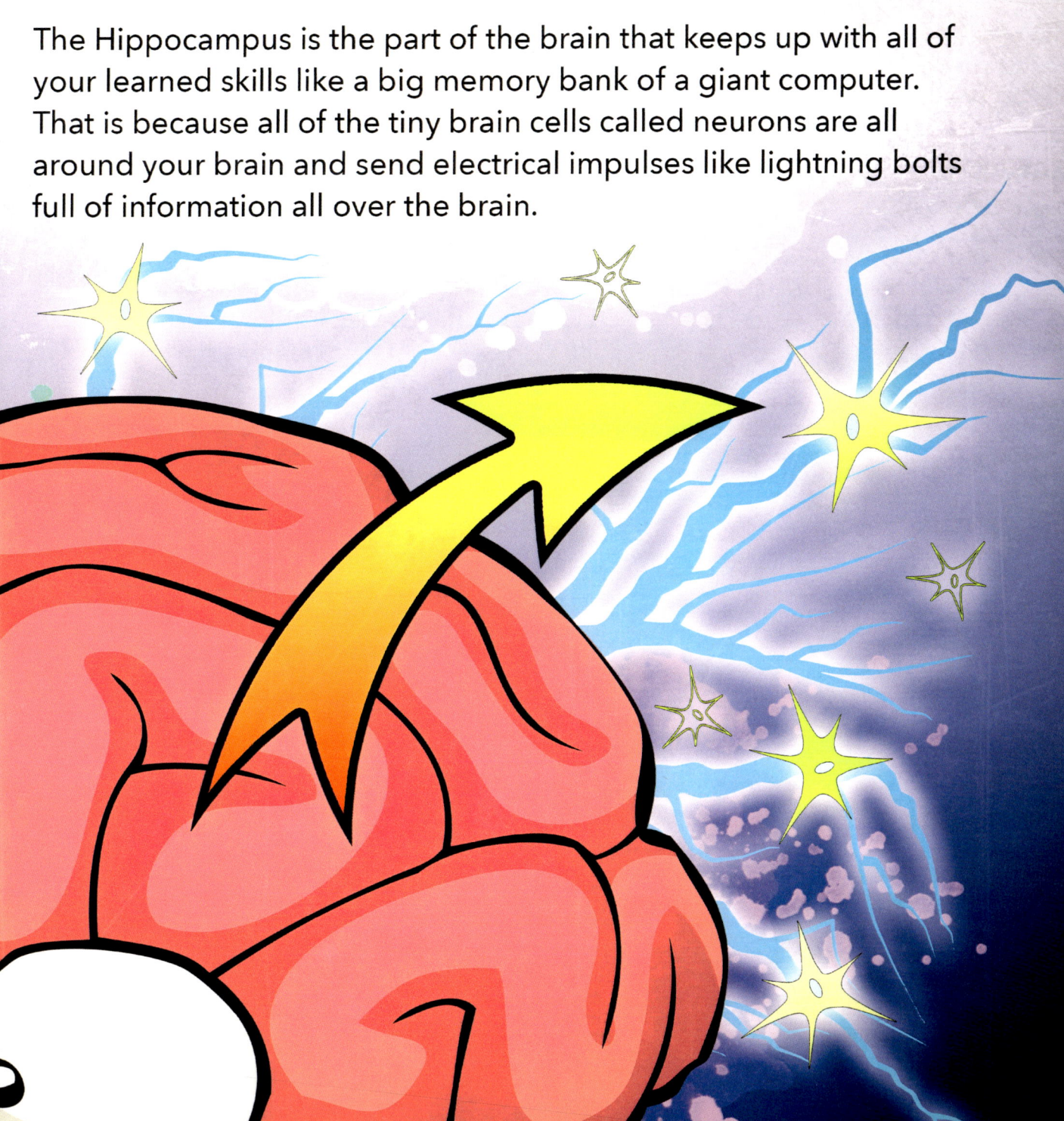

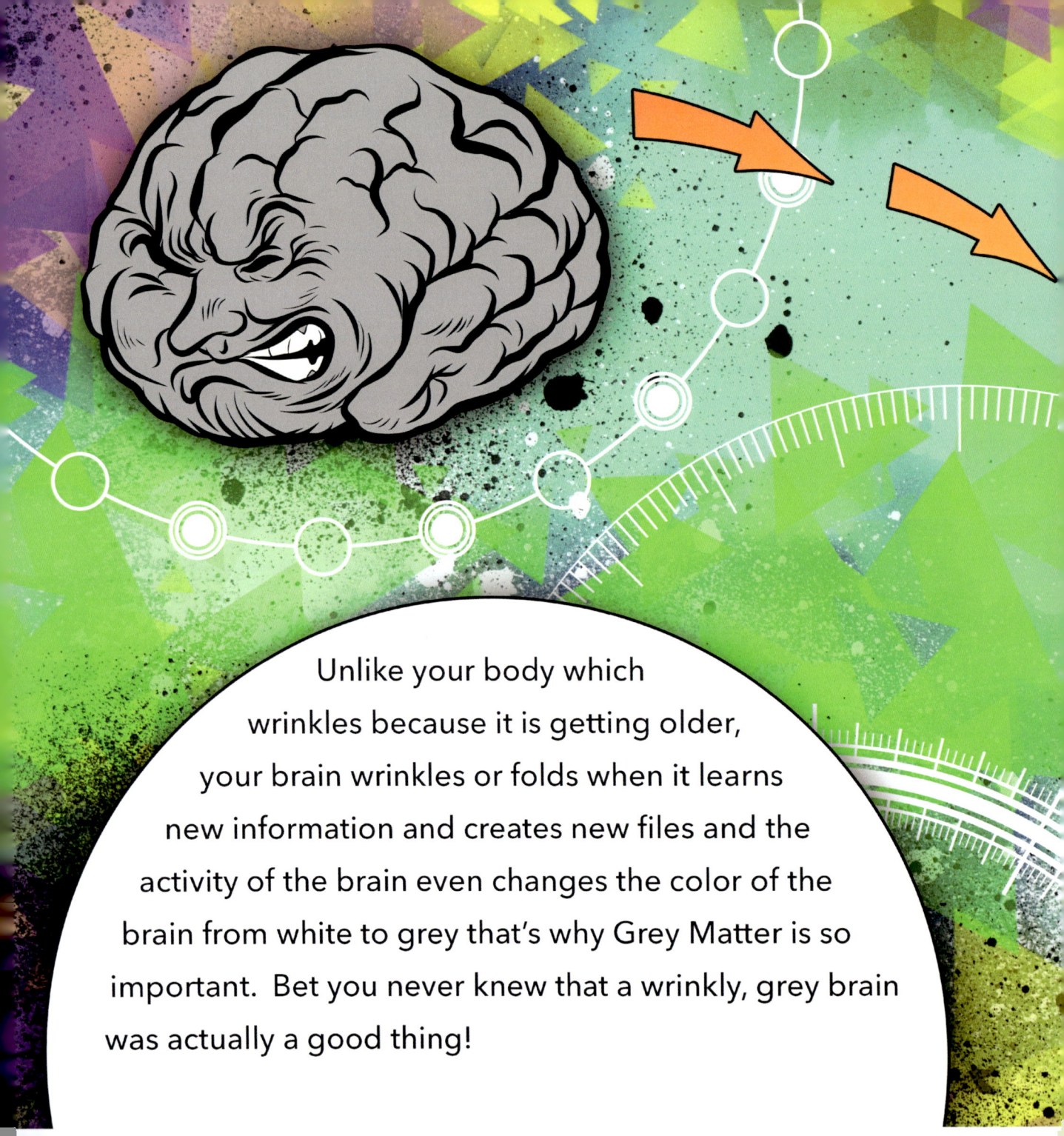

Unlike your body which wrinkles because it is getting older, your brain wrinkles or folds when it learns new information and creates new files and the activity of the brain even changes the color of the brain from white to grey that's why Grey Matter is so important. Bet you never knew that a wrinkly, grey brain was actually a good thing!

How does your brain learn?

Think about a rubber band and how the first time that you hold it, it is a little stiff but after stretching is just a little bit softer, it moves easier and you can put it around more things. Your brain is just like that rubber band in that the first time it does something, it may be hard but each time you do it, it becomes easier... that is called neuroplasticity.

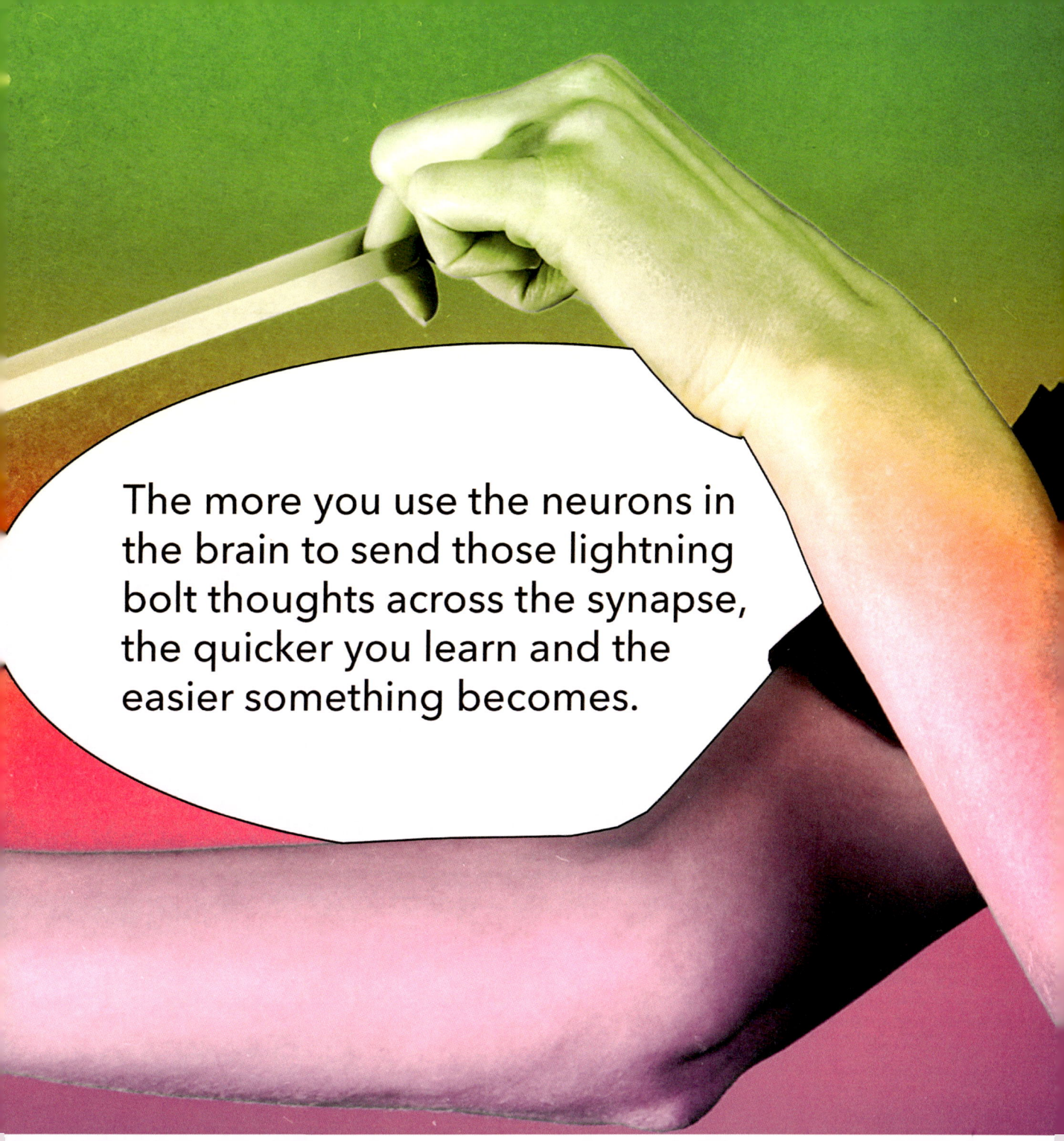

Why are mistakes important?

Even making a mistake becomes truly important because if you fall, you learn what made you fall and prevent it the next time. The same is true for a mistake, because if you fail, then you learn how to not do that and to succeed the next time.

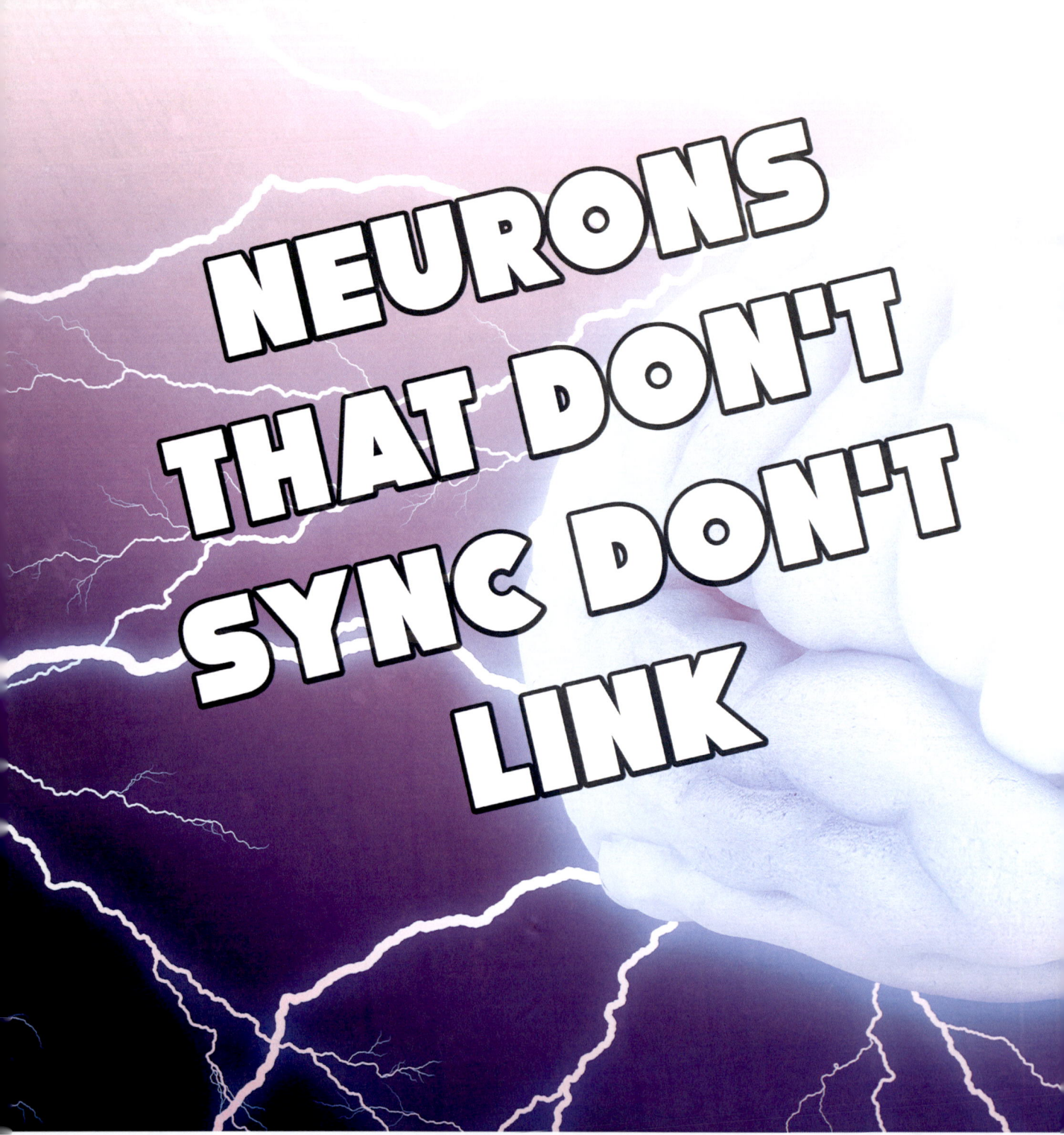

NEURONS THAT FIRE TOGETHER WIRE TOGETHER!

HOW IS THE BRAIN LIKE A SUPERCOMPUTER?

The brain is like a super-duper computer that thinks really fast, has a lot of information and sends/receives messages across a super highway to other computers. It stores great amounts of information and uses its processor which is like a very fast car that zooms across a lot of different roads and bridges, highways, small roads and even in some ditches.

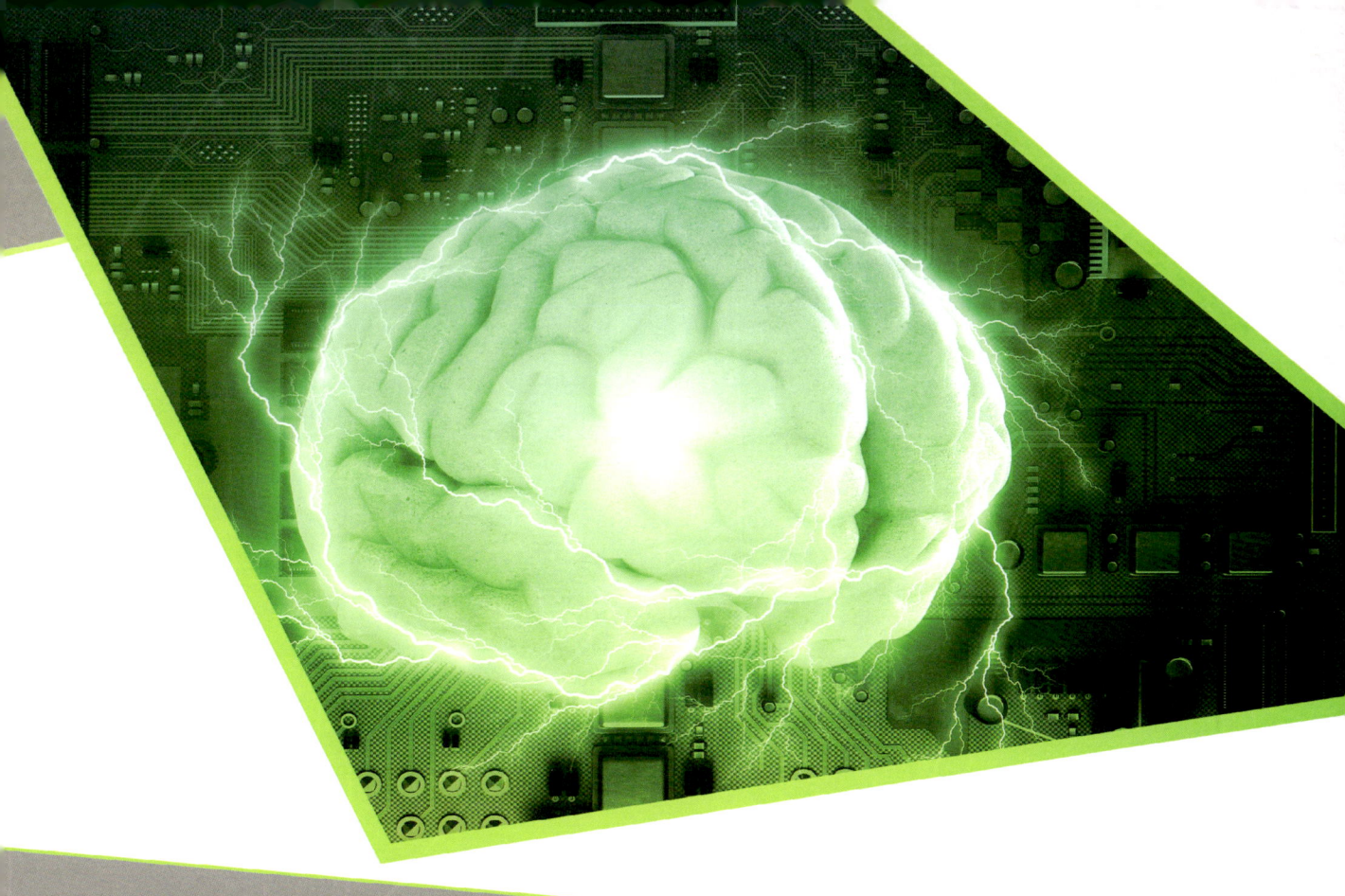

But when this super computer car wrecks, it just keeps going because it learns from the wreck and the super engine revs back up and zooms to get more information very quickly. Not only that, but the wreck doesn't even damage the car as it is flexible and malleable.

Everyone is a genius. But if you judge a fish by its ability to climb a tree it will live its whole life believing that it is stupid.   -Albert Einstien

Training your brain is important just like training before you run a marathon or swim a long distance. Knowing your strengths and weaknesses then working hard to make the "muscles" of the brain stronger through exercise helps your brain to become a champion at learning.

Doing the things that are hard makes the brain grow stronger and link new information to older information. The more linkage you have, the stronger the brain becomes and the more information it can store.

A partnership with a brain trainer can make all the difference!

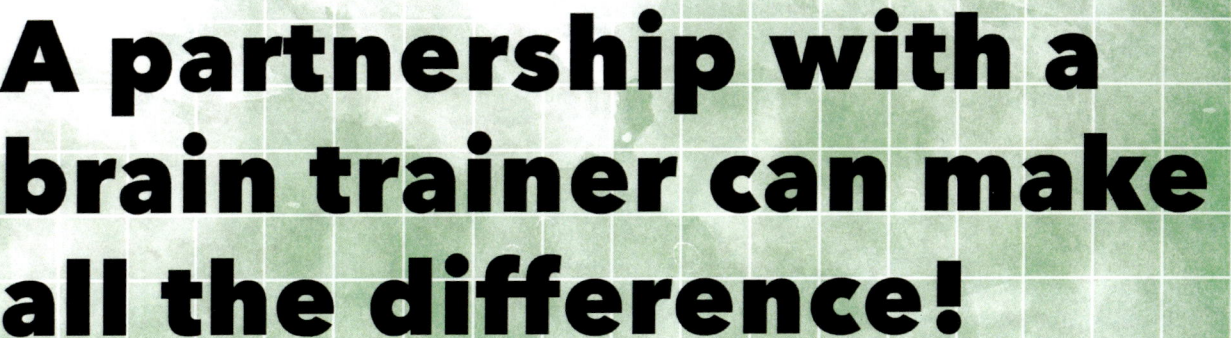

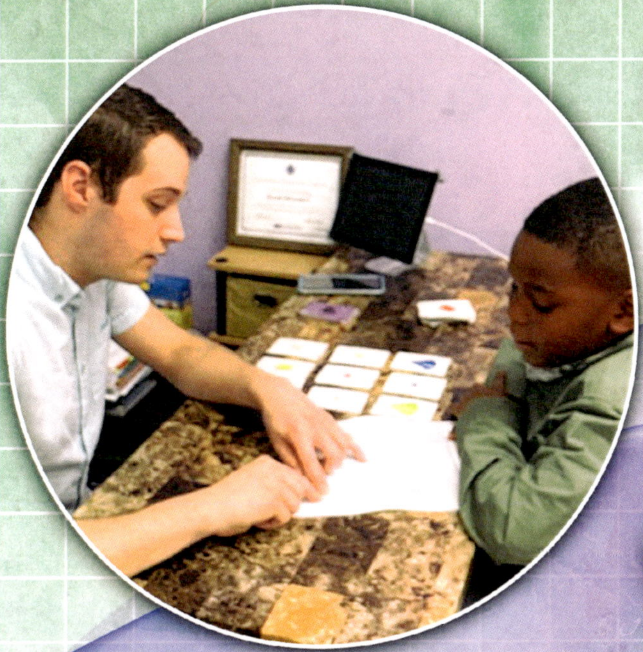

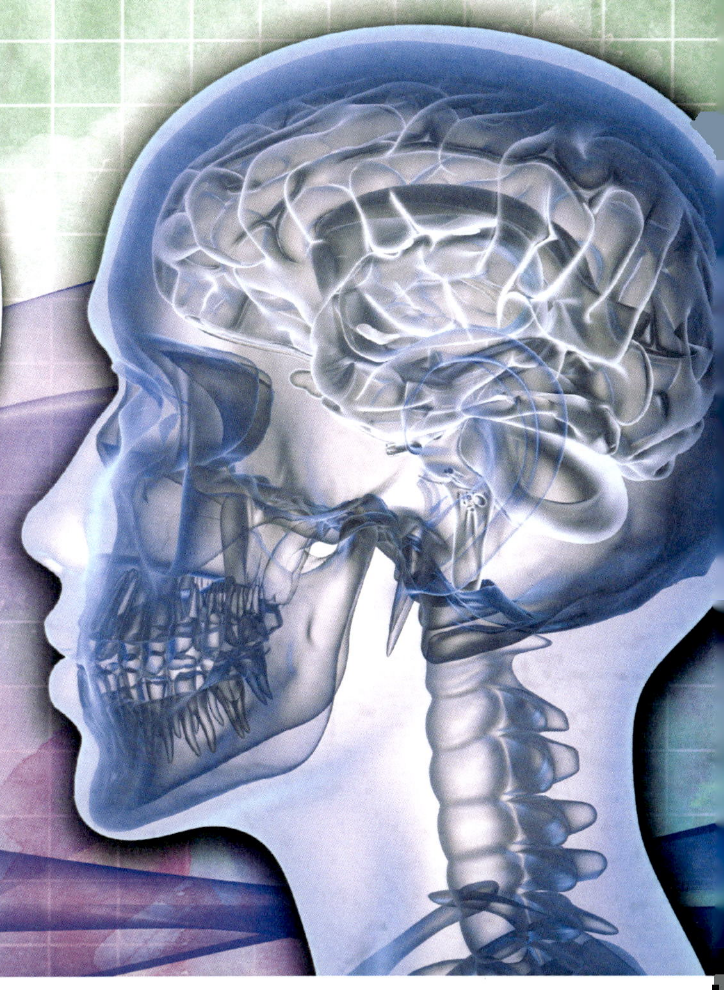

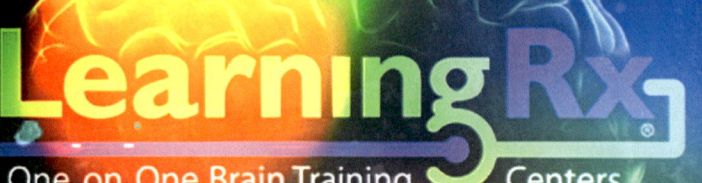

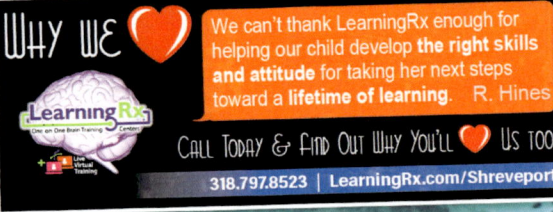

SOME OF OUR PROGRAMS.

ThinkRx®

ThinkRX is our **core program**. Offered over a minimum of 12 weeks, this program works on all the core cognitive skills. Every client who is over seven years of age and in a full program trains with ThinkRx.

ReadRx®

This program incorporates ThinkRx® with ReadRx. A powerful reading intervention, ReadRx trains the cognitive skills of auditory processing (the skill that allows the brain to analyze, blend, and segment sounds) as well as other skills that are critical to reading success.

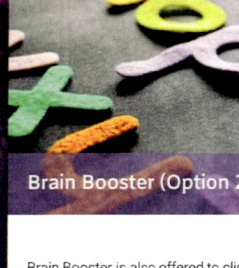

Brain Booster (Option 2)

Brain Booster is also offered to clients who have completed one of our other full programs and are interested in additional one-on-one training.

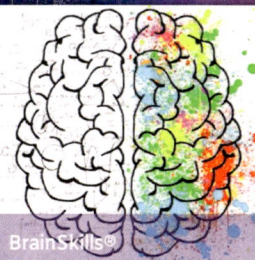

BrainSkills®

This digital brain training program that can be used to supplement the one-on-one training that is the cornerstone of all our programs, or as a maintenance program for those who have completed one of our full one-on-one programs.

StudyRx®

StudyRx® helps clients develop stronger study skills. The program teaches clients 14 test-taking tips, 12 top learning strategies, as well as eight core study skills based on fictionalized stories of historical figures and the habits, skills, and perspectives that contributed to their success.

LiftOff®

Available to preschoolers through first graders and works on the foundational cognitive skills and early reading skills so important for early learners. These include auditory processing, attention, memory, processing speed, visual processing, and reasoning.

MathRx®

MathRx® trains the cognitive skills needed to efficiently and effectively develop numerical fluency, learn math concepts, solve problems, and perform calculations.

Einstein®

Includes ThinkRx®, ReadRx®, and MathRx®

www.ingramcontent.com/pod-product-compliance
Lightning Source LLC
Chambersburg PA
CBRC102011060526
44119CB00120B/374